Youth Ministry
Bi-Vocational
Survival Guide

FULFILLING A FULL TIME CALLING
IN A BI-VOCATIONAL WORLD

RICK FLANN AND CHRIS POPE

WESTBOW
PRESS®
A DIVISION OF THOMAS NELSON
& ZONDERVAN

Scriptures taken from the Holy Bible, New International Version®, NIV®.
Copyright © 1973, 1978, 1984, 2011 by Biblica, Inc.™ Used by permission of
Zondervan. All rights reserved worldwide. www.zondervan.com The "NIV"
and "New International Version" are trademarks registered in the United
States Patent and Trademark Office by Biblica, Inc.™ All rights reserved.

WestBow Press books may be ordered through booksellers or by contacting:

WestBow Press
A Division of Thomas Nelson & Zondervan
1663 Liberty Drive
Bloomington, IN 47403
www.westbowpress.com
1 (866) 928-1240

ISBN: 978-1-5127-0043-5 (sc)
ISBN: 978-1-5127-0045-9 (hc)
ISBN: 978-1-5127-0044-2 (e)

Print information available on the last page.

WestBow Press rev. date: 04/26/2016

CONTENTS

ENDORSEMENT

What a privilege to read a book written from the heart and life of one of my "Timothy's" in the faith. Chris Pope has laid out for you the real life struggles of one who has sought to balance the responsibilities of relationships and shepherding to both his own family and the family of God while seeking to provide for his family as he is serving a church that is not at the point of providing him with a "full time" position. For those of you who are "full time" in calling yet not "full time" in position, you will be nodding your head in agreement as you read through much this book. For those of you who are blessed to be "full time" in both your calling and position, you will learn to be more mindful and sensitive to those who are having to live their lives stretched in two directions. I trust that God will use this practical book written by very humble men to speak into the depths of each reader's heart and encourage each struggling servant of Christ to "be strong in the grace that is in Christ Jesus" (2 Timothy 2:2).

Dr. Richard Brown
Associate Professor
Church Ministries, Liberty University

I have known Chris for several years now and he brings a maturity and steadiness to all he does. This book is a tremendous accomplishment and I know Chris speaks from his heart and from his experience. I'm confident that if you are considering bi-vocational ministry or simply have no choice but to be bi-vocational, this book will be beneficial.

Steve Vandegriff, Ed.D
Professor of Youth Ministries, Liberty University
Former Executive Director, Youth for Christ

Youth Ministry Bi-Vocational Survival Guide" is an excellent, much needed resource written for the unsung heroes in the trenches of youth ministry trying to live out their calling while also trying to make a living.

The majority of youth ministry is done by volunteers and bi-vocational youth workers, this book is a love gift dedicated to those faithful, hardworking people in today's church.

Dan Istvanik
7th/8th Grade Pastor
Burke Community Church, Burke,VA

Chris Pope is a dynamic and passionate speaker and pastor. He has served in youth ministry for over a decade while holding other vocational positions outside the church. Through his years of service he has had the opportunity to gain amazing insights on balancing church ministry, home and family, and serving in other vocations. This book is a must-read for anyone considering or currently in bi-vocational ministry.

Nate Richardson
Worship Arts Pastor
Cedarview Alliance Church
Ottawa, ON, Canada

I have had the honor of serving alongside Chris Pope for years in the ministry. He is "the real deal". God has truly anointed Chris with an ability to lead and love people. He is passionate about God, his family, and the ministry. I know few people that have as much integrity and ability to lead others as Chris has. He has inspired and blessed many people throughout his years in ministry, and I count myself lucky to be among them.

Practical and to the point Rick Flann and Chris Pope constantly hit the nail on the head in this guide to Bi-Vocational Youth Ministry. This survival guide comes from years of experience and will be a great text for those struggling with burnout. The advice in this book can help you refine your life back into balance and increase ministry effectiveness. I strongly recommend this book to anyone in Youth Ministry especially if your Bi-Vocational.

Isaac Terry

Youth Pastor

Deer Lake United Methodist Church

Tallahassee, Florida

I have had the privilege of working alongside Chris Pope in ministry for 3 years. In a down economy, it is more difficult for churches to offer full time employment, even when the need is ever present. This book will help those in bi-vocational ministry to follow Christ and fulfill their ministry to which they have been called.

Mark McCormick

Drama Team Leader

YouthQuest

Liberty University

Every youth pastor and staffer should own a copy of *Youth Ministry Bi-Vocational Survival Guide*. Flann and Pope are youth ministry veterans who write with the savvy of practitioners in the trenches.

Instead of painting the ideal, they lay out the real deal! You will be thoroughly encouraged by their insights and recommendations.

Keith R. Krell
Senior Pastor, Fourth Memorial Church, Spokane, WA
Associate Professor, Moody Bible Institute-Spokane

ACKNOWLEDGEMENTS

From Rick

I am grateful to the many people who God has used
to bring this book about, but above all else, thank
you Jesus for your redemption and ever-present Spirit
through the Father. May you receive all the glory!

Thank you, Tiffany Flann, for being a faithful wife who has
always been by my side no matter how crazy things have
gotten. You are the most wonderful blessing that God has
ever given me in this life and for that I am always grateful.

Thank you, Chloe, Gabe, Naomi, and Isaac Flann
for being such wonderful children who make me
proud as a dad. Jesus has lavished his blessings on me
through you. You are loved and always will be.

There have been so many people who have spoken into my life over
the years and I am grateful for every one of them, but there are a
few in particular who come to mind. Jim Harper, Kyle Schwahn
and Corey Gage, thank you for bringing me along into what it
means to be a pastor who preaches the Word faithfully. Keith
Krell, thank you for being a great teacher, mentor, and above

all, friend. Chris Pope, thanks for inviting me on the journey of writing this book; your partnership and friendship are priceless.

To the youth who I have served, and have served along side: You are awesome and have showed me what it means to be radical for Jesus. Thank you!

Finally, Thank you to everyone that I have served with in ministry. The Lord has blessed me through your presence, abilities and servant hearted attitudes. I couldn't have made it without you. Praise God for His community!

From Chris

I to am grateful to all who have made this possible. I give praise, honor, and glory to God for His love and grace on me. I am blessed and humbled at His desire to have me in ministry.

I want to thank my wife, Nicole, who has faithfully served as my partner in life and ministry. I promised her an adventure and I look forward to the continued journey. Thank you for helping me to keep my priorities in check and for loving and encouraging me on this road.

I want to thank the many students I have had, over the years. You have each been an encouragement. God has used you in my life to help shape and mold me to fulfill His calling in my life. I hope you know how much you are loved and prayed for.

I want to thank the men who have served as mentors in my life. I had the privilege to sit at the feet of great men at Liberty University. Dr. Fallwell thank you for teaching us how to cast vision. Dr. Vandegriff and Prof. Geukgeuzian, thank you for all the time spent chatting in your office and the wisdom you gave. To Dr. Brown, thank you for the years of investment. I learned so much from the hours working in your yard to hanging up Christmas lights. God has used you in many ways.

Lastly, Dr. Rasberry and Dr. Kauffman, thank you for your words of wisdom and the many lunches. I am eternally grateful for the investment.

INTRODUCTION

(Chris and Rick)

The bi-vocational youth pastor is a reality for many of us in ministry but not something we are always prepared for. A picture painted for us in college becomes an expectation. We are led to expect full-time positions, nice budgets, and salaries to support our families.

This is no fault of the colleges or professors. In fact, both of us have graduated and have served for some time in ministry. We studied under great professors and many of them had the same experiences. It is the desire of every teacher and every school to strive for the best for their students and allow them to dream.

The idea of being bi-vocational is nothing new. Paul is commonly referred to and to whom many of us are/were compared to—a tentmaker. So how do we balance the demands of ministry with our other job(s) as well as our families?

Those in ministry know there is no such thing as a part-time pastor. Crises, counseling, emergencies, deaths, etc., are not confined from nine to five. A shepherd is a shepherd 24/7.

Our desire is for you to read this book and feel encouraged and blessed. We want you to know there is a light at the end of the tunnel. We want you and your family to stay strong and healthy and not reach burnout. We want you to hear "Well done, good and faithful servant" as you step from your final page of this life and onto the first page of your next life.

Pastors must remember that Christ has set an example for how we live and the priorities we set. He was spending time with the Father while people were suffering. Christ already died for your students, so stop killing yourself or your family for them. Set boundaries and priorities that accurately reflect Christ to them.

As we write this for you, we desire it to remain a short text. If you are as busy as we imagine you are, the last thing you have time for is to read a novel. We hope this to be more like a handbook, something you can reference and easily navigate. We want this to be an encouragement and an edifying work for your ministry.

Know that you are not in the trenches of life or ministry alone. You are part of a much larger family. Thank you for answering the call that God placed on your life to serve youth. The Lord will and is blessing your obedience, even if you cannot see the seed taking root.

Our prayer for you is to live your life and ministry with the mindset communicated in the song, "Nothing to Prove," by Phillips, Craig, and Dean. "Nothing to lose, nothing to prove, and nothing to hide." This means balance in family and ministry. We are praying for you, the workers of the harvest.

So Others May Live,
Rick Flann and Chris Pope

SECTION ONE

IN THE TRENCHES

THE FAIRYTALE

(RICK FLANN)

My small children love fairytales. They want to be princesses and knights who live in castles, ride on unicorns, slay dragons, flutter with fairies, swim with mermaids, and find sunken treasure. They want fun and adventurous lives where they live happily ever after. Don't we all want that? We all want to go on great adventures, be valued, and live happily ever after.

Many of us dreamed of a day when we would be able to fulfill our God-given call to ministry. Some of us knew, even as small children, that we were called to be pastors from the first day we saw our fathers preach from the pulpit. Others of us ran as far from God as we possibly could until we realized He was never going to give up His passionate pursuit of His beloved. Still there are more who have wandered through this world knowing something was missing and never able to point out what it was until someone came along to let us know that God has different plans for our lives.

Whatever your story, we've all had—and maybe still have—unrealistic expectations of what ministry was or is going to be like. Whether seminary trained, fresh out of high school, or moving from a volunteer church position to a paid one, we usually feel as though our fairy-tale story, no matter how dark at times, is about to end as any children's story would, with a happily ever after. The problem is that children's story authors aren't brave enough to venture into the chapters that follow the happily ever after.

For the first several years of my Christian life (I became a Christian in high school), my greatest desire was to do youth ministry. I loved Jesus with a passionate zeal, but I had also made a career in youth ministry an idol of sorts.

After high school, I wanted desperately to go to Bible college, but due to some family circumstances, that wasn't going to be a possibility. Instead, I ended up heading to a Christian college in North Dakota for a year. I didn't bother attending classes consistently; I didn't give much thought to homework, and I got average grades. This didn't matter to me much because I had started a successful college ministry, studied up on faith through books that had nothing to do with science, English, or psychology, started a dorm Bible study, and led several of my friends to Christ. To me, things were great because I was "doing" ministry.

However, my perspective on ministry changed my last week of school. I had been taking a speech class and talked about Christ in one way or another during each of my presentations. I nailed them and was proud of my accomplishment. That was until I picked up my final graded paper at the end of the semester. My teacher, who was a Christian, as well as the school president's wife, scolded me for being a hypocrite in my faith since I didn't practice what I preached. I was usually late to class, missed class, did subpar papers, and it was clear I hadn't backed up what I talked about at the front of the classroom. I desperately needed this wake-up call. I had placed the sacred in front of the secular, not realizing that to God, it was *all* sacred because they were the tasks He had called me to do. Doing homework, well and on time, studying, and going to class were all acts of worship.

Unfortunately, that realization didn't stick for long. I never went back to that school and ended up bouncing in and out of community college for a few years until I finally quit school altogether. I knew God had called me to youth ministry, and in my mind, I didn't see a path there if I kept walking down this road.

With no education and no ministry prospects, I got a job working construction as a commercial framer and drywaller. This was a dark and difficult chapter of my life. I was around guys who were difficult to relate to. I wasn't naturally gifted with my hands, and I didn't see how this had anything to do with preparing for the youth ministry that I thought God had called me to. I was having doubts about the call.

I was growing bitter toward God, and my walk with Him was tenuous at best. Though He would never let me go, I was struggling to trust and follow the Lord. This eventually brought me to the place of surrender where I gave up persuing my dreams of ministry and instead, looked to the Father who knew what I actually needed, which was Him and not a career in vocational ministry. When I finally surrendered my idol of vocational ministry to Jesus, He quickly began to open up opportunities for me to serve Him in a youth ministry context. I was offered a job as a church janitor and was able to quit construction. I did a youth ministry internship, and I even went back to school to get an AA degree. The craziest part was that one day I received a phone call from one of my pastors who offered me a part-time job as the youth pastor of our church. I was floored! No Bible college degree, limited formal training, and I wasn't even asking God for a youth ministry job anymore! I was just grateful to volunteer my time to do what I was passionate about. It was as if my fairy-tale ending was about to begin. It was time for my happily ever after.

No Happily Ever After Yet!

Maybe you are dreaming of becoming a youth pastor one day or maybe you have been fighting in the trenches of youth ministry for years. Either way, we must choose to live lives surrendered to Christ each day. Once I entered into what I thought was the happily-ever-after chapter of my life, I quickly realized it was only a page that had come and gone. I didn't know how to preach. I didn't know how to organize a calendar. I wasn't sure what it meant to disciple. Counseling? What's that? Maybe those are your struggles, or maybe for you, it's the small budget you have to work with, a lack of support from senior staff, limited (if any) volunteers, or a salary that requires you to live in a cardboard box and eat rice to survive. The fact is we don't get the happily ever after until we die. Life is difficult no matter where your paycheck comes from, so it is time to wake up to that reality if you haven't already done so.

You are the reason we have written this book. We know what it's like to feel overwhelmed and underappreciated. We know that youth ministry can be a thankless job at times, and we also know that when you have countless responsibilities on top of your vocational ministry responsibilities, things can easily go from smooth sailing, to the ship is sinking fast if the right safeguards aren't in place. Chris and I have both come close to burning out in ministry and our desperate plea with the Lord is that we, along with you, would never become one of the eighteen thousand who quit the ministry each year. May these words from Paul encourage and remind us that our call is a challenging and dangerous one where not everyone finishes.

Do you not know that in a race, all the runners run, but only one receives the prize? So run that you may obtain it. Every athlete exercises self-control in all things. They do it to receive a perishable wreath, but we an imperishable. So I do not run aimlessly; I do not box as one beating the air. But I discipline my body and keep it under control, lest after preaching to others, I myself should be disqualified. (1 Corinthians 9:24–27 ESV)

Sometimes people are disqualified from ministry because of clear moral failings, but more often than not, pastors are disqualified from ministry because they have treated their call to ministry as a hundred-yard dash instead of a long and drawn-out marathon. They lose their balance, lose their strength, and can no longer run. They prioritized in a way detrimental to their relationships with others.

Maybe their families took backseat to the pressing issues at church. Maybe they were taking extra shifts at their second job, or maybe they were slacking off at their second job because it wasn't as spiritual as their church work was. Maybe they stopped spending time alone with the Lord because they felt getting things done was more important. If we don't slow down, evaluate, and reevaluate along the way, we are quite possibly going to become one of those pastors who doesn't finish the race or we will come in somewhere toward the back of the pack because we never spent the time necessary to avoid running aimlessly. We have spent too much time doing that and you probably have too. We aren't here to judge. We have also been there, and we still struggle at times to find how to best juggle the multiple things God has called us to do. Here are our stories.

A STORY LIKE YOURS

(RICK FLANN)

Happily ever after, or so I thought! Entering into vocational ministry as a youth pastor while doing janitorial work at my church was very exciting at first, and it fulfilled my desire to be in vocational youth ministry. I had come to the point of surrendering my will to God's will and was glad to do anything He asked of me, even if that meant hanging Sheetrock or cleaning toilets the rest of my life. When I was offered the job as a youth pastor, the elders of my church let me know they wanted me to go to Bible college so I would be better equipped to serve the church. I was excited about this idea because as I stated earlier in this chapter, I had longed to go to a Bible college since I had become a Christian in high school. God was now asking me to be a husband, father, youth pastor, janitor, and a full-time college student at the same time.

Not long after settling into a college routine, the worship pastor from my church stepped away from his position unexpectedly. This left an obvious void in our worship services on Sunday mornings and something needed to happen fast. At first, there were a couple of us who would alternate leading the music on Sundays, but eventually, it worked out that I was the one leading the music on a weekly basis.

I was apprehensive about taking this position, but I felt the Lord was calling me to it, as did the elders who were leading our church. So began the most crowded and difficult chapter in my life. Now I was a husband, father, youth pastor, janitor, full-time college student, *and* worship leader of my church!

At this point, I lived at a constant breakneck pace, which created some fractures in every area of my life. My wife was lonely, my kids felt neglected, church work began to suffer, school was a burden, my walk with God had become stagnant, and my passion for just about everything in life began to dry out.   There were times I wanted to quit everything. I began to imagine what it would be like to have the simple life again. I wanted things to be about me, and I wanted my fairy-tale ending to return, the one where I flew off into the sunset of perfect ministry, where things were always exciting, always refreshing, and always victorious. Or maybe I needed to flip back a few pages in the book and return to a world of fighting the dragons of Sheetrock and framing. At least then I could see my accomplishments at the end of each day, go home to a family every evening, and have a weekend. The allure of ministry had passed and the reality had settled in.

Time to Change

This is when I knew things needed to change. I had to learn how to handle the pressure or things were going to go downhill fast, but by the Lord's grace, He enabled me to better manage my relationships, school, and work overtime. I have made many, many mistakes along the way, but some steps and safeguards that I took alleviated some of the pressures that God allowed in my life for a short season. It was a time of refinement by fire, and it was through His grace that my family, ministry, and personal walk with the Lord grew.

My Story

(Chris Pope)

I have had the privilege to serve in youth ministry for the last sixteen years. I began young and it was unorthodox. I gave my life to Christ when I was twelve and shortly answered the call to ministry. I started preaching at every chance I had. I was given the opportunity to preach for "youth Sunday" at thirteen.

Shortly after, I was teaching a Sunday school class one time per month and children's church each Sunday, under the supervision of another adult. When I was fourteen, I attended a conference and heard speakers teach about God's call when I realized I wanted to do youth ministry.

Most of the churches in my community lacked having a youth ministry. Therefore, I started a youth outreach that ministered to youth in the area one time a month. We would select a different church and meet. We had a time of worship, teaching, and fellowship. After a year, we were ministering to an average of two thousand people a month. We started an online version of our ministry that spanned five different countries, and we were given radio airtime each week for fifteen minutes.

I discontinued this ministry when I went to college because our goal had been achieved. Youth ministry was now seen as important and vital in our area, and the momentum continued after I left. We had accomplished our vision. It was now time for the church to step in and the parachurch to step out.

I am going to skip ahead to when God moved my wife to Spokane, Washington. When I moved there, it became clear that I was going to have to be bi-vocational. I worked as a youth pastor, paid for fifteen hours a week and working close to thirty-five as a chaplain for hospice (end-of-life care), a busser for Red Robin, and traveled and spoke at various camps and retreats.

This was a crazy and unbalanced time. I also want to throw in that I was a full-time seminary student. It was no surprise that my family (marriage) took a hit. There was a major need for redirection and adjustment.

I resigned from hospice and Red Robin. I accepted a part-time position at a foster placement agency that had full-time potential. It allowed me to make more income to support my family. I finished school, started full time at the agency, and worked in church ministry. I limited my speaking engagements to two camps a year.

This is still busy because the life of a bi-vocational pastor is! But there can be balance. My wife is supported and my children see me as present. I evaluated my expectations and made changes. It took accountability and prayer for this to happen.

I am convinced that I need to grow in a lot of areas, but I am improving. I also believe my family sees themselves as my priority. I believe we are in a better position than we have ever been before, and this can be a reality for anyone.

Now that you have heard from us, I pray you have seen our hearts. We have in no way arrived. In fact, we are admitting the opposite; we have a long way to go. Our prayer is that you see us in the trenches along with you. We hope the following three principles will guide you along the way.

THREE PRINCIPLES TO REMEMBER

THE AUDIENCE OF
ONE PRINCIPLE

(RICK FLANN)

Leading youth ministry is much like being a swim instructer in a pool with a bunch of crazy kids. Scary, huh? You're the pro, and it's your job to save a bunch of crazies from drowning or killing one another with foam noodles and blow-up Shamu's. Your call is to teach them to swim and recruit other good swimmers to help make the pool a better place. No one wants kids to drown (except for *maybe* that one kid, because we all know that one kid), no one wants kids to wear smiley-face floaties on their arms for more than a year or two, and of course, no one wants to be the only swim instructer in the pool!   Your goal must be to disciple students in a way that will enable them to swim through this life without drowning in the deep end of this world. You are responsible to help youth move beyond their floaties of baby faith to a rich and powerful zeal for Christ. Your students should be able to not only survive in the water of this world, but they should also know God's Word and follow it with such humble competence that others are inspired to swim as you do.   Youth group should be lots of fun, but fun doesn't mean playing games for sixty minutes, relying on emotionalism as a primary source for life change, and only opening up God's Word to show kids that Jesus is coming back to kick butt with laser eyes and a flying horse. If you want the floaties and life jackets to come off your youth, do more than that. With your limited time and resources, hone in on the transforming power of God's spirit through encountering and sharing His Word. This will keep them and you from being blown back and forth in the shifting waters of false doctrine that has moved into many of our churches today.

These students should be able to swim in the direction of truth and tread water in the locations where that truth is taught and lived out. They shouldn't have to rely on you to tell them what is okay and what isn't for very long. You can always be a resource, but God's Word must be their foundation. It will free up your time and grow your ministry. God's Word will never go away, even though you eventually will.

A moment of encouragement. What I said about you being the swim instructor responsible for those kids is only somewhat true. First, remember it's only an analogy. You don't actually have to swim with them unless you're at an event or something. Swim for a few minutes, throw some of the tough guys around to establish your dominance, and then get out of the pool. Psychological victory will be yours.   Second, while it's true that God is going to hold you and I accountable for how we lead His children in the pool of this world, never forget that only God changes hearts and minds. He is the one who saves. He is the one who transforms. He is the one who brings spiritually dead people to life and grows them in the faith. Praise God that you and I don't have the power to do that because we would screw it up. We are simply called to be faithful with the things He has called us to do. We are to go and make disciples.

Problems begin when we start to place the emphasis on our own abilities, or lack thereof, as opposed to God and His abilities. We look at other successful ministries and often compare ourselves to them. We compare salaries, budgets, attendance, programs, and our time, forgetting that God has given us what He has desired to give us for this particular season of life. Our pool of students are the exact ones He has called us to serve and love. Be confident that even though God has given you other responsibilities outside of youth ministry, He has equipped you to faithfully train your students in the ways of Christ because He is the one who has called you to it, and He is the one who will make it happen.

When you have a wife, children, school, extracurricular activities, another job (or two or three), on top of what you are responsible for at the church, you have to be comfortable that you can only do so much with the twenty-four hours that God gives you each day. Don't look at your bank account, your ministry budget, the number of kids who go to your youth group, or the limited time you have to devote to that particular ministry. Look instead at the heart of God, and remember that He doesn't judge us by numbers or pizzazz. He judges by faithfulness.

In Matthew 25:14–30, Jesus gives us a wonderful picture of the type of ministry God expects from His followers. The story begins with Jesus speaking of a master who gives three of his servants different sums of money before he goes away for a long time. One of the servants receives five talents, the other receives two talents, and the third servant receives one talent. To be clear, these were not actual talents such as receiving the talent to making middle schoolers instantly quiet at the snap of your fingers. (That would be a miracle!) Talents were values of money, large values of money. In fact, each talent was valued at $600,000! So before you become sad for the one-talent guy, realize they were all given a huge responsibility and a huge blessing of trust. Right away, this should show you that God has blessed all of us with an extreme amount of God-given and God-dependent ability. They are from Him and for Him. But back to the story.

Their master had asked each servant to invest his wealth in a way that would expand *his* kingdom. The two who received the five and two talents each, invested the money that doubled their profits. The third buried his talent in the dirt, which as you know was a bad idea. Fortunately for you, the simple fact you are reading this book shows you're not one of those bury-your-talents-in-the-backyard kind of servant. By reading through these pages, you are better equipping yourself to expand God's most precious commodity—His kingdom.

When the master returned and asked his servants what they had done with the money entrusted to them, he only used one rubric to grade by—the measurement of obedience. Each of these servants had different amounts to invest, and the two individuals with five and two talents doubled their master's investment. The reward these men received was phenomenal. They received what each of us long to receive from our heavenly master one day, a "Well done, good and faithful servant! You have been faithful with a few things; I will put you in charge of many things. Come and share your master's happiness." We do not serve a God who is harsh, as the one-talent servant had accused his master of being. We serve a God who loves to see His servants succeed and longs to reward them with His blessings!

God doesn't care if you have a large or small ministry. He cares that you invest well in whatever He has given you. And that goes for *every* area of your life, because every area of your life should be viewed as ministry. Your entire life should be an act of worship. God doesn't see a difference between sacred and secular or church and non-church activities as we sometimes tend to do as youth pastors. They are all the same to Him, so how we invest into every channel of our lives will determine His response to us one day as we enter His kingdom. Walk in confidence knowing the master of the universe has entrusted you with the necessary goods that will further His kingdom. God must be your audience of one, otherwise, you may bury the very thing He has called you to proclaim. He is your only master, so walk in humility realizing it is by His power that we can do anything of lasting value as a faithful servant, even if you only have $600,000 one talent!

BALANCE PRINCIPLE

(CHRIS POPE)

It does not matter if you are full time or part time, we will all feel as though we are treading water in the pool of life from time to time. How do we strike a balance? Balance is defined as "an even distribution of weight enabling someone or something to remain upright and steady." In other words, we have to evenly distribute all the obligations in our life. Notice I did not say we had to balance expectations. No ones expectations of you, including yourself, is balanced. We need to do our very best to live lives that God sees as balanced.

Bo Boshers *Student Ministry for the 21st Century* is a fantastic resource of how to strike a balance while maintaining your effectiveness. In explaining his acronym of how to be *real*, he describes the *A* as adjusting your gauges. He explains we have three gauges: spiritual, physical, and emotional. Boshers compares the necessity of adjusting these gauges to that of a car. You have to make sure everything is balanced because if one gauge is indicating a problem, it is quite likely the other gauges are going to begin showing other problems in no time.

To balance your spiritual gauge requires you to take in more than what you are giving out. How is your time in the Word? Are you exercising the spiritual disciplines? How is your prayer life? Is it routine or is it a true conversation? Are you taking the time to listen to God? Prayer does not always require you to talk, but it always requires you to listen.

I understand that serving bi-vocationally means you are working multiple jobs while balancing family responsibilities and obligations. However, are you sacrificing your time in the Word? We know the reality of this is typically yes, and we wind up relying on our own abilities as opposed to allowing the Holy Spirit to work in our ministry. We tend to invoke the Holy Spirit in our sermons and activities while allowing Him to be cast aside in our daily routine.

We read in scripture how complete dependence on God has allowed the little to be multiplied. Why preach it and not expect it in your own ministry? He fed the thousands, and the oil jar remained full, so why would He not bless your obedience to the situation He has called you to?

Our physical gauge is one we commonly overlook. We have to take care of ourselves. We must not forget that our bodies are temples of the Holy Spirit. The tabernacle in the Old Testament reflected to the people that God was with them and our temple should reflect the same. We need to take care of our bodies as we would desire to take care of the church. Are you resting? Are you exercising? Are you eating healthy? This may sound extreme, but even make sure you go to a doctor and dentist on a regular basis. We expect people's best, why not give ours to God?

Have you ever seen a person who seemed overloaded and rundown? Picture this person taking the time to share how Christ meets all of his needs and is the best and most exciting thing that has ever happened to him. Do you think the listeners are going to believe him? Not likely! Maybe this person is you. I know for many years it was me and it hindered my testimony.

Our emotional gauge is just as important and will not be too far out of whack if the other two are balanced. Our spiritual and physical health play a major role in our emotional health. On the other hand, our emotional health can play a huge factor in our physical and spiritual as well. All three are equally important.

One way to strike a balance in this area is to take uninterrupted time for your refreshment. Spend time with your family or get away by yourself. These are just two ways to protect yourself emotionally. Accountability should also play a factor in striking a balance. Do you have a person you can trust to help you sort out your feelings and point you back to the promises and commands of God?

BALANCING ALL
THE ABOVE

(CHRIS POPE)

Striking a balance in life will help you persevere and stay the course. These gauges are important because they require you to have a balance in God, family, work, and ministry service. Notice the order of words in that sentence.

God has to always be your first priority. You would think this is a given, but we all know from experience just how quickly we forget. As pastors, we are more prone to confuse our relationship with God and our ministry for God. We must avoid this area. Crossing this line makes us Pharisees!

Our family is an undisputed and vital part in our ministries. Could it be that family is our primary ministry? We have all heard, in some way, if we fail at home, nothing else matters. It is not just a cliché, it is reality. At school, I met too many people who did not want to be in or marry someone in ministry because of how life in ministry was demonstrated to them as a child.

For many pastors, the church is the mistress. Although not a hidden one, she is there. Nothing is worse than an open affair! If that is not bad enough, we are surrounded by people who push that mistress on us. We know affairs tear families apart, so why not take the extra steps to avoid it within our own home. Look at a picture of your wife and a picture of your kids, are they not reason enough for balance?

Part of protecting and balancing our families is to keep God first, as we stated earlier. This is spending time in the Word, praying, practicing the spiritual disciplines, taking a Sabbath, etc. You are demonstrating to your family, wife, and kids what your focus is.

Next comes our wife. We have to love her like Christ loves the church. My wife needs to know I love her more than I love the church, more than I love my children. She needs to know this to feel safe and secure. I not only demonstrate who God is as a Father to my children, but also as a husband to my wife. My life reflects Him by my love for and service to her. As I meet this need for her, she is an extra blessing in my life as a pastor. She enhances my ministry.

It is easy to say our children are our lives. It is hard to see them otherwise. We love our children before they take their first breath, but I had to grow in loving my wife. It is hard to strike a balance here; however, it is vital we do so. My children need to see what a proper relationship is by how their mother and I live it before them. In a world where more than half of marriages end in divorce, they need a sense of security. Do we forgive? Do we show grace? This vital piece is missing from many homes.

I want my son to learn how to be a father by watching me through example. I want him to trust the love of God because he trusts me. I want him to learn how to be a man of integrity and character by watching me. This cannot happen unless I make my son a priority.

If you notice, I put work after family and before ministry service. There is a reason for that. I remember starting as bio-vocational, still am, and feeling as though my ministry needed to come before my secular job. I mean, wasn't I called to be a pastor? However, I am now convinced I got this wrong. My first ministry is to my family and to provide for them. If I am slacking at my secular job for the sake of ministry, I am sacrificing my family for the sake of ministry. I am building a disconnect in the DNA of my family, ministry, and life. I am also hindering my testimony and not serving God to the best of my ability.

Ministry service is our service for God under the umbrella of a local church. This includes sermon preparation, preaching, staff meetings, parent conferences, student and parent counseling, going to student activities, having lunch with them, planning events, discipling them, etc. Obviously, there are more items I can add to the list, but you get the idea.

Again, we know there is no such thing as a part-time youth pastor. We have part-time compensation with a full-time job description. It is easy to see so many needs, get caught up, and start sacrificing. It is easy to come up with many excuses as why this is acceptable. This is where a continual reminder of our priorities is important. You can start by listening to your wife. Sometimes what we see as having a supportive wife can, in reality, be a wife who has come to believe that "things are what they are, and there is nothing that can be done about it." This is dangerous!

For example, for some reason I thought it was a great idea to take not one but two seminary classes the month before my son was born. Or when I planned our fall kickoff two days before his due date. My wife never complained, never said anything. What I eventually realized was she had feelings about it, but I never let her voice them. Instead of being my partner in ministry, she was a bystander.

You may know by now I am a Type A personality. I have lists and charts, and I pride myself in my organizational skills. Even in this, I can fall prey to having things out of sync. It is important to evaluate your life circumstances. I had a leader who would go away for a weekend with her husband every six months and they would evaluate their family. They would talk about their kid's activities, the spiritual health of the family, goals for their family, goals for their marriage, etc. It helped them stay on track and keep the main thing, the main thing. When she told me this, it was a breath of fresh air.

I desire to do something similar. Remember, what works for some families will not always work for your own. I sit down several times a year and examine my family, my spiritual health, and family goals that my wife and I have set. I check to see if there is something unbalanced in the equation, but also to be proactive to busy periods that we know are coming up. We are not always perfect, and we have failed at this many times.

For many youth pastors, summer is a busy time of year. I am blessed to have some flexibility in my secular job that allows me to work from home quite a bit. Since I know the summers are busy, I work from home three days a week and am at the office two days. This allows me to be home with my son. Knowing his personality, this is a major benefit and blessing for him.

So what is going on in your life? Are you working multiple jobs? Are you expanding or starting your family? Are you newly married or going through the motions? Are you going to school while working? You can evaluate many more circumstances. I encourage you to sit down with your wife or your fiancé and evaluate your priorities. For those who are not married yet, it is difficult to change when you have always done things in a certain way. Make changes now; your future wife will appreciate it! Meet with married couples and ask them what has worked or has not worked well for them. Job shadow a pastor and see how he interacts with his family and the church. Spend time with people who are farther down the road of life than you are, and watch to see what is or isn't balanced in their lives.

Setting these priorities and making changes establishes a great precedent for your family. You are building a legacy and reproducing yourself into another generation in your own home. What better feeling is there than that?

Therefore, it is important to assess the needs versus the wants of your family before you accept a position. If you feel God is calling you to a church, and it is not full time, look at your family circumstances, evaluate the needs, review the job description, and have an honest talk with the leadership. Go into it with your questions ready and your concerns known.

I had the privilege of serving at Liberty University's Center for Youth Ministry's departmental ministry team, YouthQuest. I met my wife there, and had the ability to help train future leaders as we ministered alongside one another. After five years, God was calling me to Spokane, Washington.

Cornerstone Community Church was honest with us regarding salary. It was not much and it barely covered rent. However, they were taking a step of faith in hiring a youth pastor and trusted God would provide. They gave me a full page and a half job description. They knew this was a description for a full-time position. They wanted me to review it and realistically tell them what I could do.

My wife was working at the time, and we had not started our family We looked at where we were and what I could do. We set priorities for the youth ministry and for ourselves. We endured bumps along the way, but God blessed the ministry, the church, and us! The church was very supportive. Whenever there was a need, a loss of income, or a child added to the family, the church blessed and took care of us.

Money should not be the deciding factor, God's leading should. If you are obedient in following Him and leading your family, your needs will be met. For example, two months after we arrived at the church, we could not make rent. We told no one! We prayed, and when I returned home from work a week later, there was a note on our door from an anonymous family who told us they had refinanced their home and used the extra money to pay our rent. Thank God!

I encourage you to take the time to determine what balance looks like, evaluate your circumstances, and set realistic priorities. It may mean a slower beginning, but will result in a fruitful end.

I want to take a few minutes to expound on an earlier topic—adjusting your gauges. Since we are talking about balancing, I want to talk about the spiritual gauge. This is the one area that pastors often neglect because they are overconfident. You might not realize, but every time we neglect fostering our relationship with God by replacing it with something else, we are demonstrating prideful self-reliance. We will sacrifice our quiet time and substitute it with sermon preparation. We won't clear our minds and remain focused, so we will read scripture and think of how we can turn it into a sermon. How often do we fail to communicate with Him in prayer as opposed to telling Him what we need? We are going to hit on a couple of these topics.

Spiritual Disciplines

The spiritual disciplines are those acts that aid in us becoming more like Christ. It is a sharpening time in our lives, the inward and the outward disciplines.

Examples of inward disciplines are prayer, fasting, memorization of scripture, journaling, etc. The outward disciplines can be demonstrated in public worship, public prayer, public service, etc.

Numerous resources are available that can help you understand more of the spiritual disciplines.

Exercising these disciplines helps Christianity move from becoming something we do, to someone we are. We, as pastors, need to be the same at home as we are anywhere else. That includes our secondary vocation. We become better employees and our reputation and testimony builds. We will also become more of the family man we are supposed to be. When everything else is in alignment, ministry seems to go much better.

My wife taught me a humbling lesson when we were dating. When we were engaged, she fasted two times a week until the day we were married. She was working full time and going to school. She was just as busy as I was, but our marriage was so important that she fasted for it. God knew we needed it. It was a humbling experience and I am forever grateful.

Bible Study

This is the most important factor in growing in your relationship with Christ. As a believer, a husband, and a father, this cannot be neglected. We excuse our lack of time in the Word with how busy life is: sports, family activities, fatigue, etc. We wind up using the same excuses we hear from our students and get frustrated by them. C. H. Spurgeon once said, "Study yourself to death and pray yourself back to life."

I recently asked my students what they were most passionate about. I asked them how they knew it was a passion. All of their answers demonstrated an action. So consider then our relationship with God. Does our life reflect it as a passion? Why or why not? Too many pastors stumble and fall because the Word of God becomes a matter of the mind and not of the heart. Don't fall into that trap.

I can understand how your time in the Word could be hindered because of obligations. But if it is something we want bad enough, we will make a way for it to happen. Consider spending fifteen minutes each day and then select one day to do more of a study (an extended time). Use a solid devotional or read a chapter or two, and then follow up with a more in-depth study later. Make sure you lead by example. How often do we tell our students that life will just get busier? What are we waiting for? If we do not take the time now, what makes us think we will take the time later?

If you commute to work, you can always listen to an audio Bible or a devotion. There are multiple methods to make this work. It takes time, prayer, creativity, and accountability. Many cities have several gatherings of youth pastors whom you could build a relationship. If you like to workout, you could always listen to sermons or devotions on your iPod. It may not give you the adrenalin rush, but you are being fed. What is more important? For those who are married, consider utilizing the blessing of your wife. My wife is very wise and has much to offer. This is another way to make her a partner in ministry and not a bystander. Our families desire to be our biggest advocate. Trust them with what needs advocating in your life.

Prayer

I stated earlier that "prayer does not always require you to speak, but it does require you to listen." How often do we wish our students would focus and give us their undivided attention? Should we not give the same to God? God knows my heart and its needs before I can even form the words.

As I rush from one meeting to another, or drive from one side of the city to the next, I can call someone, listen to music, or pray to God. I would recommend getting a small pocket-size notebook to write your prayer requests. It is also good to keep enough blank space to jot down when they were answered. This serves as an encouragement and reminder of what God has done. It will also increase your prayer life and makes it become a discipline.

Another avenue to consider for you planners out there, create a chart with a spot for each day of the week. You can divide various prayer requests up on a particular day. This can help you give more devoted time to some requests while accommodating your lack of time.

If you use social media (what youth pastor doesn't!), take advantage of the technology by creating a youth ministry prayer page or a youth ministry prayer e-mail. It bridges a gap between you and your students, and it creates a simple venue for sharing prayer requests.

1 Thessalonians 5:17, says, "pray continually." So many times we live as though prayer is an interruption to life as opposed to life as an interruption to prayer. We must do our very best never to let that be the case. This is something we must strive for. It will never be perfect, but this is something we can improve.

One of my favorite ways to stimulate prayer is to set alarms on my phone. I was recently helping a ministry get started, and there were few people stepping up to serve. I was reading Luke 10:2 and encouraged everyone to set an alarm on their phone for 10:02 a.m. as a reminder to pray for workers of the harvest. It was a hit with the ministry and very fruitful. Find ways to set alarms for specific requests. This is something I still battle on a regular basis, but I don't do this because I have to, I see it as my response to understanding what God did and continues to do for me. Sometimes we simply need a reminder.

We have given you some examples on how to implement the spiritual disciplines in your life and ministry. As valuable as those are, scripture makes it a point to show the value in having partners in ministry. It is important to have these men sharpen us as we do what God has called us to do. We each need to seek these three men in our lives.

—

Paul, Barnabas, and Timothy

We need these three men of scripture to model after in our lives. We all need Paul (teacher), Barnabas (encourager), and Timothy (disciple). I never had these people in my life when I first started, and it was not until I was a college student that this became a reality.

My Paul was Dr. Rich Brown. He saw me as a person who had a hurt past and needed to be raised up and sharpened. He took me under his wing and taught me how to be a man of character and integrity. He mentored and encouraged me. He helped make me the pastor I am now. We did not always agree, but we agreed on whom we lived for. I would assist him in everything from grading papers, having meals, yard work, and hanging Christmas lights.

My Barnabas was Andrew from New Jersey. He saw me as an equal, and I valued his honesty and friendship immensely. Rarely had I enjoyed such a genuine friend. We all need someone who is not going to judge us, but encourage us with truth. Scripture refers to the trustworthiness of the wounds of a friend. He told me some hard things, but I knew he loved me and cared about my current and future ministry. I am forever grateful for his friendship.

A Timothy should be a natural part of our ministry. However, we can go overboard in this area. As a pastor, we should be discipling students. However, we need to assure balance. I made the mistake of wearing five different hats and trying to disciple seven different students a week for one and a half hours each. I was drained! I would recommend that you disciple no more than three students, and maybe start with one when you are part time. Encourage other leaders to disciple and spend more time teaching them how. You need to have Timothy, but you need to have something to give.

THE ACTS ONE
PRINCIPLE

(RICK FLANN)

Imagine for a moment being one of Jesus's twelve disciples after He had risen from the dead. You went from feeling as though you had been played a fool who followed a dead counterfeit savior to a disciple who was full of joy at the undeniable fact that your Savior had actually turned out to be the risen King! Not only that, this God walks through walls, cooks breakfast on the beach, and teaches you and your friends about how, from the very first verse in Genesis, all Scripture points to Him as being the Christ, the Savior of the world, Jesus.

If I had been one of those twelve disciples, I would have wanted to parade Jesus around from town to town showing everyone the holes in his hands and feet and proclaiming He had risen from the dead. I would have Jesus walk through walls, and I would definitely remind people that I had followed Jesus *before* any of them did because I was one of the original twelve.

I hope you can see how heretical that all sounds, but I want you to grasp something important from this silly idea of a disciple parading Jesus around. Could it be that this disciple sounds more like you and me than we realize? How many times have we done something totally dumb because we didn't rely on the Spirit of God to direct us? Do we pray before and during our message preparation? Do we evaluate what the students in our ministry need, or do we simply follow the latest trend making its way through the church? Do we ask God whether we should take that extra speaking engagement even though it happens during your wedding anniversary or on your child's birthday? Do we plead with Jesus to keep us authentic in how we live out our lives for Him? Our agenda must never trump His agenda.

If we don't evaluate constantly and pray fervently, we will end up looking foolish, and Christ will not be seen for who He truly should be in our lives—glorious. Though Jesus walked with His disciples for forty days, He never had them hold any "reach the world for Jesus crusades" during that time. It was a time for Him to train His disciples to go and make disciples all over the world, but it wasn't time for them to actually implement the plan. Had they tried it, the disciples might have actually acted as foolish as I had made them out to be in the beginning of this chapter. Here is why. In Acts 1:4–8, right before Jesus ascended into heaven, He ordered them *not* to go anywhere until the Father had given them a gift. This was no ordinary gift as you could imagine. It was a gift of the power and presence of God abiding in each one of them—His Holy Spirit.

If you are a Christian, the Spirit of God abides in you. Period. Let's not get caught up in terminology here (filled/baptized, whatever). The fact remains that God is in you, God is with you, and God will never leave you or forsake you. The one who holds the entire universe together by His will has chosen to take up residence in you and me. No matter what our circumstances are, the God who overcame the grave is molding us to be more and more like His son,

Jesus, every day, "… for it is God who works in you to will and to act according to His good purposes" (Philippians 2:13). Unless we are operating in the power of the Spirit, we should wait and do nothing. Otherwise, we will be operating in our own strength, which will amount to nothing of eternal significance.

In Acts 2, after receiving the Holy Spirit, the once-cowering Peter preached to such a large crowd that three thousand people were saved when he presented the gospel to them. There was no sermon prep, there were no PowerPoint presentations, and there was no sound system to project his message to the masses. It was undeniably God doing the real work. Peter and the disciples were faithful, but it was through the power of the Spirit working in and through them that made all the difference.

It needs to be the same for us. Most of our families aren't impressed if we can teach them the Bible in Greek or Hebrew. But they will be moved if they watch us diligently read God's Word and pray on our knees regularily. Or what about at our secular jobs? Do we fast and pray for those whom we work alongside and who don't know Christ? The apostle Paul sets a great example for us to strive after in Romans 9:3 when he says he would be willing to give up his salvation so his Jewish counterparts might come a saving faith in Christ. A mindset like that can only come through the Spirit of God working in our lives, but is one we must strive to have.

What do we do now? We must always find our confidence in the work and power of God dwelling inside of us and His working through us. Jesus said it in Acts 1. Wait on Him, rely on Him, and trust in Him. Have no confidence in yourself. Put all of your eggs in one basket, and look to God to provide your every need. We must abide in Christ because there is nothing about us that is adequate for living a life that makes God look great. We must depend on Him.

SECTION THREE

FINDING THE SWEET SPOT

Making the Most of What You Don't Have: Time!

(Chris Pope)

Our desire is for you to have some practical tips to get your mind rolling on how you can set reasonable boundaries to protect your family and your longevity in ministry. We have a mentality that everything rises and falls on our availability, skill set, and personality. Who do we think we are to believe we are that important? How often do we feel no one is stepping up or we are alone? Could it be because we are not getting out of the way? Is our ego that controlling?

None of us are that important. We need to make sure that in everything we do, we are pointing people toward Christ. If I have a leader who is more equipped to handle a situation or conversation, I encourage my students to talk to that person. If a student has a similar interest as another leader, I encourage a relationship to foster. At this point, I become a leader reproducing other leaders.

Despite this, there are still areas that, as leaders, we need to grow in. There are boundaries we need to set for the betterment of our families. We are going to look at some common ways to show your family that they are your priority. It is important for your family to see it, but also for your students to know it. They need to see an example of a stable family.

This section is an attempt to give you practical help in balancing family, work, and ministry, and have some sense of structure and organization.

Phone

All of us have a phone and most of us have a smart phone. I am not sure about you, but this can be a major distraction for me. There is a positive way to look at it; most smart phones have this little feature called Do Not Disturb. It is a great feature that allows me not to hear noises from my phone from eight o'clock in the evening until seven o'clock in the morning.

I had a coworker whose daughter made a wish for her birthday that her mom would not answer her phone. This is not something I want to experience. I do not want my children to dread my job; I want them to be proud and support it. I let my students know the boundaries and most of them respect it. I let them know I will only respond if it is an emergency.

With the in-an-instant mentality, we should discuss texting. Just because someone sends you a text, does not mean you have to respond right away. I follow that principle with students, pastors, and my other places of employment. Ninety-nine percent of the time, it is something that can wait. However, there will be those times in which an emergency will arise.

E-mail

I would recommend having a separate e-mail account from your work. The temptation would be to cross the two, as many do. When I separate my account, I am able to limit who receives that address. This enables me to set a point person with my work address when I am going to be away. If there is a situation that this person cannot handle, he or she can get in touch with me. I will only respond to this person.

Make sure you utilize an away message for e-mails that generate an auto response. This frees you up from feeling as though you are leaving people in limbo and helps alleviate stress.

Something to consider is, and could seem a stretch, is applying the 1 Corinthians 10 mentality here. Just because something is permissible, does not mean it is beneficial. Just because you can have your e-mail appear on your phone does not mean it is necessary to have it turned on. I have my e-mail programmed so when I am away from the office for an extended period, excluding vacations, I have access. Other than that, it is turned off.

Time

We have made marriage a repeated theme in this book because we know how important it is! Ministry is not a nine-to-five job. You will have to adjust your schedule for your family as you do for your students. If I am away on a Saturday for a youth trip, I will take another day off to make up for it. If I have youth group on Wednesday night, I will either start my day later that day or the next, or I will get off early. I would express to your supervising pastor the importance of family time and establish some boundaries. If he or she is not open to it, mention this desire during your annual review.

Schedule

Scheduling is important and oftentimes overlooked and underrated. When you look at creation, we see God is a God, or order, not chaos. We should model our lives the same way. Our priorities are revealed by looking at the calendar. I recommend you sit with your wife at least twice a month and compare schedules. Consider inserting your wife's appointments in your own.

Make sure you are carving out uninterrupted family time. Consider using a paper calendar. It is so easy to use a digital one and accept everything that comes across your screen. When you have to write an engagement down, it makes you consider if it is worth the time.

If someone wants to plan something with me, I respond, "I am sorry, but I do not have my calendar with me. Let me check, and I will get back with you." This response allows me to discuss it with my wife with little pressure.

I would also recommend writing all family events in ink. It causes the event to stick out in your mind while demonstrating the importance in your eyes. It shows commitment. I would always tell my students, "There is not a single person who lacks commitment, the question is, what are you committed to?"

Vacation

The first thing is to take one! You can have a "staycation." That simply means you stay in town and do local things. It can be fun, exciting, and smothered in quality time. I recommend turning off all technology.

Pretend you are at a cabin somewhere. Inflate a pool in the backyard, put up an umbrella, make Popsicles, play music, hang lights, and have a blast. Pretend you are not responsible for the upkeep (you would not be able to if you were away). There is time for it later. Make it a fun and exciting experience for your family. Allow them to help plan the theme and use their imagination. Check and see what is around town: local parks, pools, lakes, and campsites, etc. Vacations should not equal bankruptcy, they should equal quality time.

Just Say No!

I am not referring to drugs here. I am talking about not feeling obligated to accept every request from every person who comes your way. Just because you are a pastor does not mean you are a doormat. Sometimes we need to say no to good things and say yes to better things. When we fail to say no, we hinder someone else from saying yes.

Many things will come across your desk that seem like once-in-a-lifetime opportunities. When I start to get bombarded with various ideas, I have to remind myself that David wanted to build the temple. God said no. It was a great idea, but it was for someone else to do. David simply had the privilage of setting the stage for it to be done.

Precious Moments

Being busy is a reality. That is why it is imperative you be intentional in making special moments for your family. It shows how much you care and that you put forth the effort. It can be as simple as a game night, a daddy date, getting ice cream, or wrestling on the floor. Make sure you spend quality time with your children, both together and individually. As long as it is time with you, it is precious to them.

Every Saturday I take my son, Noah, on a daddy date to get ice cream. I can honestly tell you it is the highlight of his week. He asks for it constantly and wants to make sure we are still going to have the date. It warms my heart to know this is so special to him.

LEADING IN
THE LEAN

(RICK FLANN AND CHRIS POPE)

I recently had a conversation with a pastor starting a church in town. The pastor was convinced we needed to compete with the world. Many would agree. We do not. I want a ministry that is totally different from the world so there is no comparison. That is where life-changing decisions are made.

Churchleaders.com recently had an article by Francis Chan where he stated, "Last summer, I came to a shocking realization that I had to share with my wife: If Jesus had a church in Simi Valley, mine would be bigger." Why would he say that? Because he realized people go to churches where the commitment is easy. Jesus repelled people and we attract them. Be careful you don't compromise the message with your method.

My spiritual gift is that of a prophet. What it means is that my strength is to see things in black and white. My weakness is to see things in black and white. I have had former students say they never liked other youth groups because they were entertained and not challenged. I had a small number leave my ministry because there were not enough games. Upon leaving Cornerstone, my students asked me to find a replacement that would teach the Word.

SET THE DIRECTION

(CHRIS POPE)

This can be a difficult topic for a youth pastor. So much rises and falls on this one thing—direction. There are numerous texts on the subject, and just about all of them sound attractive. We can sometimes be tempted to merge ideas or borrow from another successful ministry. In many ways, this is a form of fraud. Your ministry needs to be an original.

We have to be careful we do not compare the successes and failures of our ministries with other churches. People are different and therefore the needs are different. I have a number of books on the subject of successful ministry, and I made the mistake in trying to implement all the listed principles. The result was a strained and disfunctional ministry. One book, *Simple Student Ministry*, stood out and radically changed my way of thinking.

I realized I needed to scale back. I became guilty of overworking the youth ministry and trying to make it appear like so many others. My church already had a vision and I was blind to it.

Think of it this way. What is the mission and vision statement of your church? The answer to that is also the answer to the mission and vision of your youth ministry. We unintentionally breed division in our church. Most youth ministries, mine included, were/are guilty of treating our youth ministries as separate churches.

Our youth ministry should be an extension of the church. The same focus for the main church should be universal for the various ministries of the church. In doing so, it becomes a stronger body and each ministry supports the other.

When I realized I was working separately from the rest of the church, I sat down with my leaders and shared with them how I was struggling. We spent time in prayer and sought to develop ways to get back on track. Our pruning process had begun.

Years ago, I had the opportunity and privilege to meet Dr. Jerry Falwell of Liberty University. I had a dream for a future ministry, one I am still hoping to see happen, and someone suggested I share it with him. I went into that meeting not knowing what to expect or even what to say. I was a nervous wreck.

I was amazed at how humble a man he was and his conviction concerning what God had for him. He was always famous for starting every school year with the same story of how Liberty was founded. We could sit there and mouth the words along with him of how he walked across this property as a kid and convinced the owner, years later, to sell it to him for God's university, one that would train champions for Christ. I have never forgotten that story, and it encouraged me never to quit.

I shared my dream with Dr. Falwell, and he patiently listened as I spoke. He was kind and encouraging. Toward the end of the meeting, he asked, "What can I do for you?" I asked him how he knew Liberty would happen and how he got people to believe in it. His reply has always stuck with me and is something I have told many people since, "People buy vision, not ideas."

When making any type of change in your ministry. Either getting back on course or changing direction altogether, we must first believe in the vision and then truly cast it. People need to buy into it, believe it is possible, and know they can help get it there.

BUILD GOD'S TEAM

(RICK FLANN)

When I first became a youth pastor, I used to sarcastically joke to my wife that it was the Rick Flann Show at every youth group. I did the setup and teardown, ran games, led the music, and preached the message; essentially, I did just about everything. Some might say I was a superstar for being that multitalented, but that wasn't the case. I actually didn't do any of it very well and found myself completely exhausted at the end of each youth event.

I quickly realized if I was going to survive at all in vocational ministry, I was going to have to distribute the load to others. The church is the Body of Christ and according to Ephesians 4:11–12 "… he gave the apostles, the prophets, the evangelists, the shepherds and teachers, to equip the saints for the work of ministry, for building up the body of Christ." If God was calling me to be a shepherd of His people then I was called to equip them for the work of His church. The Bible is very clear that we as youth pastors, especially bi-vocational ones, are not called to do everything. In fact, we are called to create an environment where others are able to use the gifts God has given them for the furthering of His kingdom.

Don't ever get stuck thinking you have to do it all. You can't, nor will you ever be able to. Churches are notorious for giving part-time pay with full-time responsibilities, and for you to survive, you have to build a solid team to support you and the ministry. This is nonnegotiable. If you don't build a team, you will burnout or get fired and potentially hurt a lot of people along the way. Here are some things you can do to avoid this pitfall.

Pray!

This may seem obvious, but if you are honest with yourself, chances are prayer is at times a neglected part of your life. Most of us youth pastors are doers. We move first and ask questions later. This can be good at times, but it can also get us into trouble. When it comes to building God's ministry team, you better pray, ponder, and reflect on what it is God wants you to do and how He wants you to do it. We tend to see prayer as an interruption to life and all its demands as opposed to seeing those demands as an interruption to prayer.

Develop an Application

One of the first things I did to move away from the Rick Flann Show was develop an application for every potential ministry leader. You can't afford to simply go on blind faith. There is too much at risk. Your student's spiritual growth and physical safety are too important to risk by allowing an unqualified or potentially dangerous person to lead them.

Make sure to do a background check on every person who applies. Include several essay questions that force applicants to think deeply about their lives, their call, and their faith. Also, have a reference section and actually contact the people on the list. Each of these things will allow you to get a better feel for where they are spiritually and enable you to ask questions you otherwise may not have thought of. I have also found that roughly a quarter of the people interested in helping in youth ministry don't ever return their application to me because of its length. That's perfect, because it shows that they wouldn't be willing to invest all that much in the young people of our church.

In addition to filling out the application, I have two in-person meetings with the applicant. The first one is where I present the application and gather some general information. I also ask if that person has any questions for me. Once the individual has completed the packet, he is invited to come to youth group for two to three weeks to see if it's something he believes God might be calling him to. From there, we have our second meeting where we review the application. The background check has been completed and references have been contacted. By doing this legwork ahead of time, you will have saved yourself a great deal of trouble in the future. At first, I was fairly lax in my choice of leaders. If the person had a testimony, a clean record, and a heartbeat, I would take that individual. Eventually, I honed my questions in and was able to get a sense of their love, or lack thereof, for youth ministry. Resist the temptation to take anyone and everyone who wants to join your team. Don't exclude for exclusion sake, but do be careful. An unqualified leader might offer you a sigh of relief for a short season, but will eventually suck more of your time and energy than it was worth, and the consequences can be devastating.

Keep Your Head Up

Always be on the lookout for people who God may want to use in your ministry. God is notorious for using those who are unassuming in their appearances. Don't automatically think the flashy person as being the best person for the job. Above all, look for the Godly person who knows the Bible and doesn't have an allergic reaction to anyone under the age of eighteen. Continually ask the Lord to show you who you may be overlooking, and ask Him to put situations in front of you that might guide you to the right individuals.

Take Some Calculated Risks

Once you have some leaders by your side, it might still be tempting to do everything by yourself because you can do things better (or you might think) than the people you have added to the team. Eventually, this mentality will stifle things because leaders are there to lead and not watch you. Let them do things. Take some risks. Let your leaders ruin a game or two, mess up announcements, or forget to refill the snack shack supply closet.

You were once there, and you still are from time to time! Lavish your leaders with grace and train them in the ministry. Youth find it endearing, most of the time, when you and your leaders make the occasional mistake, and it keeps us dependent on God. In the long run, the youth ministry will grow in depth and breadth because of it, and you will gain some time back. Plus, the more personally invested your leaders are, the more likely they are to stay.

Treasure Your Leaders

I can't overstate this one enough. Besides God, your leaders are the life of your ministry. Treat them like it! If you have any budget at all, spend the majority of it on your leaders. Maybe you have no budget. Then get creative. Write your leaders a note and have your kids draw them a picture. Have them over for dinner. Have someone in the church bake them a cake and sing an off-key happy birthday song to them on a youth night.

Each year, I have leaders write down what they want for their birthday. One of them loved Reese's, so I bought them a Reese's mug off eBay and filled it with Reese's candy, which ended up costing a total of six dollars. Another leader loves Star Wars and Legos, so I bought him a Star Wars Lego keychain for five dollars off Amazon. You get the idea. Making someone feel valued does not equal big bucks or lots of time. Expand your communication with them and their communication with one another. Create a private Facebook page for leaders where they can share prayer requests and praises for them and their students. It's also a great place to keep everyone updated on what is going on in the ministry outside of e-mails.

We also have monthly leader meetings where we review ministry and eat a meal provided by some people from the church. We usually make our way through some training material I have developed or found off a website, or we will study a book together. Whenever we go through books, I will buy each leader one, but if that isn't an option, I make some photocopies of the pages that matter the most and hone in on those. To save a few bucks, I never buy new books, but instead buy used books off Amazon or eBay that are marked in excellent or good shape. My leaders know money is tight, and they appreciate the materials and value them. Remember, above all else, use your budget to invest in your leaders. This will improve the ministry and eventually free up your time because it creates a self-sustaining culture.   Meet with your leaders. Pray for and with your leaders. Invite them over to eat dinner with your family. Bring them along in your normal day-to-day activities. Train them through your actions. Challenge leaders to do the same with their students as you do with them. Create a culture of service and investment from the top down. You will find more leaders will desire to serve in greater ways and carry more of the load as you disciple them in the ministry.

Find Their Gifting

You want your leaders to fire on all cylinders, and one of the ways you can do that is by helping them to learn how they are gifted. There are plenty of personality tests that can help. As spiritual as it may not sound, learning how to navigate different personality types can really help in the messy world of ministry. Also, it is very helpful to have them take a spiritual gift test. God has gifted us to fulfill specific roles in this world, and knowing how we have been equipped is important. Ask your leaders what they are good at and what makes them feel passionate. If a leader enjoys statistics, see if he or she would like to track students' attendance. If one loves acting, see if she might want to run games. If he has a passion for evangelism, see if he would take some students to a homeless shelter. The more you know about the individuals, the more you can set your leaders free to do the work of ministry, and in turn, teach them to do the same.

Train Leaders to Train Leaders

As this discipleship mentality becomes a more grounded part of your ministry, it will spread and develop more fully. In the youth ministry that I run, we now have a youth leadership team that helps run things at both our Sunday service and midweek meetings. Look for the potential in the students that God has placed under your care, and give them opportunities to serve alongside you and your leaders. I have made plenty of mistakes in ministry, but one of the best decisions I ever made was creating a youth leadership team after establishing a solid adult leadership base. Students are willing to do just about anything and have a zeal many adults lack. They can set up and teardown chairs, be greeters, run a snack shack, make announcements, run games, lead music, and even preach at times. The key is that you and your other adult leaders walk alongside these students in the process. Again, this may take a bit of work up front, but the long-term payoffs can be huge. It took me about three years for this to happen with any level of lasting success. I tried to start a youth leadership team the first year I was a youth pastor. It was an epic failure. First, I still didn't know how to manage myself and the couple adult leaders I had because of my inexperience. Second, I hadn't yet developed a structure where I could invest that type of energy. Third, I didn't have the material, time, or know-how to do a good job. Finally, my motivation was to be like the big church youth ministries instead of Christ's youth ministry. Eventually, I shelved the idea for a later day. I would reccomend you treat this concept a bit like a leadership pyramid. At the top is you, then your leaders, and then the students. Of course, invest in students individually, but for your ministry to have the greatest influence with your limted time and resources, spend the majority of your energy on youth adult leaders. This will eventually free you up and empower them to develop student leaders who help run things. Of course, you must care for your own soul above all else. If that lacks, so will everything else.

Hard Conversations

Being a leader requires you to make hard decisions at times. Sometimes a person who made it through the application and interview process just isn't cutting it. Make sure you are in communication with that individual, and you are doing whatever you can to help that person fit into the culture of your ministry. But sometimes things don't work out and you have to let someone go. Yes, it can be uncomfortable, and yes that person might not like you for a season, but you don't have time to keep an unqualified leader around. That person is there to help and not hinder. Be patient and spend time in prayer, but at the end of the day, realize you can't afford to keep someone around who is detrimental to the ministry.

A Reminder

As a final note for this section, remember every situation is unique. Evaluate everything in light of where God has called you to be. Take one step at a time to implement change and let your leaders in on it. Slow strategic steps take time and will allow you to do things better over the long haul, which will also spread out the load you carry.

Focus on the Essentials

(Chris Pope)

There were many great things about serving at Cornerstone. The church had a great mission statement and it was reiterated every year. The church summed up the focus of the church in three simple statements. We exist to Love God, Love People, and Change Lives. These simple statements help guide me to have a functional and influential ministry.

These three statements absorbed everything from evangelism, to discipleship, to outreach. The purpose of this section is to help focus on the essentials in ministry. What do you do well? What do your leaders do well? What about your students?

We have to remember that despite the training we have, we are not the only ones who can serve. My students knew I would go to their school and have lunch with them. However, they also knew I would *not* invite their friends to youth group.

It is essential in our student ministry that the students reach their peers and learn how to do it as early as possible. I have not earned the right to speak into their peers' lives. They have! Their friends are likely to respond if they are asked. Our students saw the affect of inviting their friends. When they started taking the initiative, we saw the youth ministry grow both deep and wide. We saw thirty-five students come to know Christ this last school year. We have had fifty in the last two years.

So let that serve as an encouragement not to see yourself as the only implementer in your ministry. Students desire to be challenged. Students desire to serve. Remember, people buy vision, not ideas!

When I sought to get back on track with the church's overarching vision, I had to be creative and give a visual. I created a chart to aid with this. The first image was the blank chart each leader received to complete. The second one was what we accomplished to scale back and strike a balance. It looks simple and may appear lacking; however, knowing the needs verses the wants of our students and developing a plan has proven very effective.

Xtreme Impact Think Tank

This is to help develop ideas to change our methods without compromising our philosophy of ministry.

1. Events- Activity presented in a short period of time on a specific day (sports events, food events, lock-in's)
2. Marathons- continuous, multiple day events (Retreats/ Camps/ Missions Trips)
3. Series- Continuous weekly/monthly events (Sunday School; Wednesday Night/ Discipleship/ Leadership Team)

Levels	Events	Marathons	Series
Level 1 Pre-Evangelism			
Level 2 Evangelism			
Level 3 Growth			

Level 4 Leadership & Ministry	_____ _____ _____ _____	_____ _____ _____ _____	_____ _____ _____ _____

Xtreme Impact Think Tank

This is to help develop ideas to change our methods without compromising our philosophy of ministry.

1. Events— Activity presented in a short period of time on a specific day (sports events, food events, lock-in's)
2. Marathons— continuous, multiple day events (Retreats/ Camps/ Missions Trips)
3. Series— Continuous weekly/monthly events (Sunday School; Wednesday Night/ Discipleship/ Leadership Team)

Levels	Events	Marathons	Series
Level 1 Pre-Evangelism	Fall Kick-Off		WED Night Program Hang Time
Level 2 Evangelism		VBS Winter Retreat Golden Broom	Prayer Walk
Level 3 Growth	Lock-In	30 Hour Famine HS Retreat	Discipleship Summer Bible Studies
Level 4 Leadership & Ministry	Backpack Give-a-way Christmas Give-a-way	Missions Trip	

This served our students very well over the years. It also gave leaders a realistic view of what we expected. It helped the leaders prepare and reinforce the mission and vision of the church and ministry.

The far left column represented the four levels of ministry that we categorized every activity. The goal was to strike a balance. All the activities were listed as an event, marathon, or series. Our goal was to have the youth ministry be manageable for parents, students, and us. The parents saw this as a sign that I wanted to partner with them and help them and not become something else on a calendar.

Whenever students or leaders wanted to do an activity, they had to justify it by telling me where it fit in and whether there was already something we were doing that accomplished the same purpose. If it was a repeated purpose, we either had to replace it or say no. It built balance into the heart of our ministry.

I have a friend who lives by the mantra, "Go Big or Go Home!" It is catchy, funny, and applicable in many areas in life. Youth ministry does not have to be one of those areas. Sometimes we need to trim the fat. We need to say no to good things so we can say yes to better things. Life is hectic for most of our students. Let's not complicate their faith as well.

TEACHING ...
IN A CRUNCH

(RICK FLANN)

When I was a young boy, I used to dread just about everything having to do with going clothes shopping, except for one thing—the rotating door at the front of the store! It was like a small adventure for me. I would see the doors spinning slowly, and I would try to squeeze through them just as my window of opportunity to pass unscathed was closing. I was like Batman, except I was not as cool as he was, so the door would sometimes win the battle.

We all know what it's like to feel the crunch of a deadline. It's not comfortable, and when you are in ministry, deadlines seem to come up a lot. Church work is like a rotating door. It's an adventure, but if we play it too tight with our time, we are going to get smacked. For many of us, we are on a weekly rotation of sermon preparation. Without fail, as soon as youth group ends, it's time to prep for a new sermon.

The Lord has given you a very important call as a pastor, and as part of that call, you are likely to preach His Word on a regular basis. According to the Bible, you are held to a higher standard in how you live your life and how you rightly teach His Word. You must not neglect this area. It should take a higher priority than anything else in the ministry should because it is foundational to Godly effectiveness. You and your leaders could be great facilitators, but if you don't teach the right doctrine, you are a cult. I have senior pastor friends who spend upward of thirty- to thirty-five hours a week in message preparation. This doesn't mean you must spend countless hours in study for sermons if God has not given you the time to do that. Thirty- to thirty-five hours a week for message preparation probably doesn't describe your situation, and it doesn't describe mine either. So the question is how can we honor the Lord through our message preparation with a limited amount of time and resources?

Be Organized

Most youth pastors struggle in the area of organization (including myself). You can usually tell where the youth pastor's office is not by the sign on the door, but by the mess on the desk. Get it together. Have someone who is naturally organized help you structure things in a way that will allow you to be more effective with your time. Have a daily or weekly clean-the-office routine. It's usually one of the first things I do after wrapping up youth group for the week. If you don't have room to work, you won't be as focused as you should be when it comes to writing your message. Don't waste time looking for papers you know are "somewhere in here." Don't bend the spines of your commentaries because they slipped off your old pile of camp registrations, and don't kill your brain cells by leaving rotting food in the drawer. Clean equals effective and that means a better youth ministry and a calmer mind.

Some of you might argue that messiness helps you with creativity. I used to make that same argument, and let me tell you how blissful it has been since leaving the dark side (even though I go there for a visit from time to time). Give organization a try, please. Cleanliness is *not* Godliness, but I think it might come close.

Know Your Resources and Know How to Use Them

I love downloading music. When I was growing up and I really liked a song, I bought the cassette or CD and hoped the rest of music was as good. In downloading music, I can select what I want and leave the rest. Beyond that there's often that helpful "listeners also bought" section. This allows me to view other artists whom I would have otherwise never heard.

We live in a time when there is more information at our fingertips than we can begin to know what to do with. The key is finding the resources that will help you in the preaching of the Word (among other things). Just like with the "listeners also bought" on song sites, figure out what other ministry workers are doing. What preachers do they love to listen to? Expand your listening list. Read blogs, books, and websites. What pastors influence you? Find some solid commentaries (there are some great free ones online). Listen to youth ministry podcasts. Read articles about how to structure and deliver sermons. Find illustrations. Expand your grid, as it will have a positive influence on your messages and help you with the creative and theological elements you need for effective teaching. Another vital part of message preparation is spending some time with others who are in the trenches of ministry. Have coffee, make a phone call, send an e-mail, walk to your senior pastor's office. Ask questions. Get feedback. Look at how and why they do what they do. Ask how they prepare their messags, and ask them to look at yours. If you are brave (be brave, it's worth it), see if they will come to your youth group to evaluate how you spoke and how you run things. Almost every time I'm preparing a message, I ask trusted friends what they think about certain aspects of it. If I'm stuck on interpretation or I need a good illustration, I ask for their thoughts. Usually, I walk away refreshed and moving in a better direction.

It might sound like these things will take up lots of your time. That doesn't have to be the case. Listen to sermons or podcasts while you run, drive, or are doing simple work (like organizing your office). Have your wife, student, or a friend read from a ministry book while you are driving or having some downtime together. Spending an hour or two each month with another person who is fighting the same ministry battles as you are will energize you to do the ministry God has called you to do. Remember, we are after effective-time management that leads to more time available.

Refine Your Style

As important as it can be to enrich ourselves with the resources around us, never forget that God made you to be you. There have been many times that I have been able to pinpoint who a pastor's favorite preacher is simply by listening to him speak for a minute or two. You are an original, so embrace it and refine it to your advantage. Just because you read something, hear something, or like something doesn't mean you have to replicate it.

When I was in Bible college, I was taught how to prepare sermons. This was obviously a good and valuable thing. The problem was these methods were sometimes as scripture. There is a right way and a wrong way to prepare messages, but there is also room for some freedom. Don't feel trapped by people's opinions, rather, feel freed by biblical constraints, the truths that never change.

Develop your own style. If, for example, you only have two hours a week to prepare a message, become familiar with the Scripture and context you are going to teach, and go straight to the commentaries, if necessary. Don't feel obligated to peruse every Greek or Hebrew word in the passage. Focus on the timeless truths of Scripture and let it do the talking. Don't forget that God has called us to be faithful to the things He has given you and that is all that matters. Make sure to evaluate yourself after you speak and include others in the process. This will help you become a more effective speaker and will, in turn, free up some of your time as you develop.

Also, develop a pattern for the notes that you use to preach from. For example, I highlight my main points in bold and underline them. I italicize Scripture references and make them red. I indent in different distances to signify certain things. If I have an example or an illustration, I mark it **EX:** or **ILL:** (bold and capitalized). I have developed my own preaching preparation and style over the years. This has allowed me to become more effective with the time that I have allotted toward my weekly message preparation.   I encourage you to take a few minutes (yes, right now) and head to joshharris.com and search "preaching notes." You will see how Tim Keller uses a code that looks like gibberish, Matt Chandler peppers his papers with handwritten notes and a highlighter, and how Mark Driscoll only uses a couple sticky notes attached to his Bible as aids.   Now that you have seen firsthand how the pros don't fit that cookie-cutter pattern we were taught in Bible college or from books, experiment and become comfortable in who you are as a presenter of God's Word. Discovering how God has gifted you in preparing and giving messages will help you become a better preacher. You will enjoy it more, you will be better at it, and you will become more effective.

Procrastinate Appropriately (maybe just a little)

Right off the bat, this one isn't for everyone nor should it be, but for some of you it might offer a bit of needed freedom. Notice I said freedom and not entitlement. I will not say it is best or even good to procrastinate. However, there are times where we are left with few other options. Sometimes, when that rotating door is about to close in on us, we are at our very best.

The other week, I was speaking at our children's church summer camp. Circumstances came up and I had very little time to prepare. I crammed in what I could and when I could. I stayed up late and woke up early. As the week progressed, I was able to complete the messages quicker and found a groove that would have been hard to find had I slowly worked through them in the months prior. Sometimes, God forces us into uncomfortable situations to train us and keep us dependent on Him. Other times, we find ourselves in difficult situations because we have not been faithful in managing our time well. It's important to do your very best, and when the craziness comes, trust that God will supply everything you need to make Him look great.

Find your sweet spot. For example, I don't work on messages for the upcoming week on Fridays because my mind is tired and dreaming of a day off. I spend that time working on camps or events, calling students, organizing, or working on worship music keynotes. Don't procrastinate for procrastination sake; be smart in how you use your time. But when those times of pressure come, use them to your advantage. God will give you everything you need even if it might not look exactly how you want it to look. Allow these times to push you deeper into your relationship with Christ, and watch Him turn you into a more effective communicator for Him.

Share the Load

God's Word was here before you, and it will still be here once you leave. Don't think because you are the youth pastor it means you are the one who always has to preach. I felt like that at first, but quickly realized if I was going to survive the ministry with all of the other responsibilities that were on my plate, I would have to allow other qualified individuals to teach occasionally. This is one reason why training both adult leaders and students is so important (in that order). If there are people around you who seem to have a gift for speaking, and more importantly, have a faithful walk Christ, see if they might be interested in preaching. Sure, you will have to work with them, but that's great! You are discipling and you are setting yourself up to have a few more hours available from time to time that you can dedicate to other things.

Also, connect with other ministry leaders. See if an elder or pastor from your church would be willing to speak occasionally. Ask a trusted saint from your community group, Christian school, or a fellow youth pastor from another church to come and speak to your group. I do this occasionally with our youth ministry and the payoff has been huge. An added bonus is the students will usually pay more attention to the guest you bring in to speak because it's something different. Try it and you will see.

You Won't be the Best but That's Okay!

There will always be someone smarter, better looking, and funnier than you and I are. It's the reality of life, and you better come to grips with it. The sooner you realize God has made you in His image for purposes that He has in store for you, the sooner you will be able to stop beating yourself up about how you don't sound like all of your favorite preachers and youth ministry gurus. Be you. Find your confidence, rest, and joy that you are a redeemed child of Christ created in His image.

You might not be a big conference speaker, and you might never lead an eight hundred student youth ministry, but it doesn't matter! Our job is simply to be faithful to the things that He has called us to. Some of the wealthiest and most sought-after people in heaven will not be the famous preachers, but rather the lowly janitors who cleaned up after them.

Protect Your Time

As mentioned earlier, pencil in all of your appointments, except for your family time. When it comes to message preparation, you should almost always do the same. Write it in pencil, but do everything you can to avoid erasing these times from your planner. Keep them consistent each week. Dedicate your best work time to preparing your messages. Studies suggest we do our hardest mental work at the beginning of the day because our brain muscles become tired as the hours go by. God's Word must not be neglected for a needy student, a cranky parent, or a frustrated board member. If they want to meet during your message preparation time, let them know it won't work unless it is an emergency. Even then, if there is something major going on, it probably did not start in a day, and a single meeting right then probably will not solve it either. There is almost nothing worse than being unprepared for or winging a message. If you remove these times from your calendar, you may never get another chance to work on it during the week, which is likely to make it less powerful. God may still do some amazing things, but He will let you fail at times if you have not honored Him in how you prioritized your schedule.

Teach Expository

Many styles of preaching and many schedules can be followed when it comes to sharing God's Word. Generally, these can be broken down into two categories. The first is topical and the other is expository. Topical preaching is self-explanatory. You pick a topic and then fit Bible verses into your message to support the points you are making. Expository preaching is typically less practiced in the youth ministry culture. In its simplest form, expository preaching is when you allow the Bible to teach for itself. You don't pick where it goes, you let it pick where you go. This happens when you preach a book of the Bible from start to finish.

I am not saying either is right or wrong. They both have their advantages, but I have grown to love expository preaching. I am confident it keeps me more faithful to the text. I still do topical series occasionally, but going through the Bible one book at a time has become routine for me. Here is why. Expository preaching saves me time. I don't have to spend lots of energy planning what I want to talk about each week and then find verses that support what I have to say. The Bible tells me what's next because I need to look at the next few verses to find out where to go.

I don't have to hunt through lots of different resources to find information I need for the message. If I have a budget for books, I only need to buy one or two commentaries or find some free ones online. These will remain valuable resources to return to even after you have moved on to the next teaching series.

When you do expository preaching, students will be able to see and experience how they should read and study their Bible. When I ask a student what he has been reading in the Bible and he says, "Well, Rick, I opened my Bible to Philippians 4:13 today, and God showed me that 'I can do all things through Christ who strengthens me,' I figured I don't need to study for my tests anymore because I can do *all things!*"

First, I attempt to restrain myself from saying something snarky to the kid about how I hope he gets an *F* so he learns to read his Bible correctly. Then I kindly let him know that Philippians 4:13 has nothing to do with being a slacker, and instead, has everything to do with embracing each situation that God puts you in, no matter how challenging. In reality, he should be the hardest-working student around.

Do you see how context matters, and if we ignore that then so will our youth? If I do expository preaching, I can bring them back to that and how we should read the Word of God in the same way. Like I said, topical and expository preaching are both beneficial at times. I get that it's hard to do a Vision Series while doing expository preaching. The biggest factor is allowing the Bible to speak for the Bible. If you are looking to save time and direct youth in a way that will naturally point them to right Bible interpretation, work on expository preaching. It won't gain you cool-guy points from some in youth ministry, but it's not about them anyway.

Counseling

(Chris Pope)

Six years ago, I had a student approach me after a message I had given. She was distraught and I was shocked. She seemed like she had it all together. She was funny and outgoing. All the students wanted to be around her. Clearly, something had upset her.

I preached on our bodies being a temple of the Holy Spirit. I spoke of how God dwells in our bodies, and we need to take care of them. I emphasized how much God loved us and His temple. I thought this was encouraging, she thought this was devastating.

In front of the stage and with tears in her eyes, she raised her shirtsleeve and showed me her arms. They were covered in cuts and scars. "How can God love this?" she asked. I was stunned and recognized the guilt she was feeling. I quickly said a prayer asking God for wisdom.

"What do you see when you look at your arms?" I asked.

"Scars, nothing but scars!" she replied.

I asked her what scars were. She said it was a healed wound.

"That is right," I responded. "It is a sign of healing. God wants to do to the inside of you what He has done on the outside. He wants to make you whole."

This time she cried for a different reason.

I wish I could say that was the end of the situation. However, the door had just opened. She was female and I could not counsel her. It would not have been appropriate, so I referred her to someone else. We need to keep this in mind when counseling students. We do not always have to be the ones to counsel.

When I interview leaders for our team, I ask them about their personal past struggles; things they battled or areas they have experienced. I do not do this to embarrass them or cause them to relive situations. I do it so I can best refer a student in a similar situation. If the issue is resolved, the leader is better able to point the student to the right scriptures and share strategies on the road to recovery. It builds a natural discipleship and accountability relationship.

Many reference guides are helpful when working with students on various issues. If a student made an appointment to see me, I would quickly brush up on my understanding of his or her particular issue. However, there comes a time when you need to refer out or bring someone else in.

It is easy for youth pastors to bear the burden of their students, but it is unhealthy for them and their families. You can walk with your students, but you cannot carry their load. We are there to pray for, pray with, encourage, laugh and cry with them. Unless you are a professionally licensed counselor, it is best not to act like one.

The help we can give is oftentimes limited. I would include another leader who can help and has some type of experience. See if your church knows of a counselor who you can run by a hypothetical situation. See when it is best to refer. Involve the parents, unless safety is a legitimate concern. Many times, our role is best as a support, sitting second chair, than it is as the primary caretaker. This is especially true for those of us who are bi-vocational.

We have talked about the limited amount of time for those of us who have to work multiple jobs in addition to our calling. Because of our necessity to work, we cannot let what happens in the lives of our students hinder our performance in other obligations. Yes, you are called to ministry, but you are called to provide for your family. Don't sacrifice them for the sake of ministry. There will always be ministry, but what does that matter if we have failed our family? What are we teaching our sons and daughters about ministry? Be men of integrity! If you are bi-vocational, work your hardest, and pray for your students as you work. However, pending a life-threatening emergency, don't compromise your other obligations. At that point, you are compromising your family.

Jake grew up in a broken home. He was struggling with some life choices and receiving advice from peers, Mom, Dad, pastors, etc. I took him to Subway to talk. I sat there as he told me of his conflicting thoughts, what everyone was saying, and how overwhelmed he felt. Jake is a student who I care deeply about. In some ways, he was like a member of my family. I simply asked him, "How can I best help you? What do you want from me?"

He said, "You're doing it. You're here."

Sometimes for students, just knowing you are there is all they need. I found when I identified the limits of my abilities, and when I needed to include someone or refer out, it created safe boundaries for my family and myself. It also allowed me to be in a more supportive role for my students. It strengthened our relationship.

As a part-time youth pastor, I was limited on time. Therefore, I had to find ways to interact with my students so they knew I was accessible, while at the same time, respecting my family time. I use text messaging frequently. It allows me to see if students want to chat or if something else is going on with them. If it is just to chat, I inform them I am spending time with my family, and I will catch up with them tomorrow. If it is more than that, I briefly continue. I will see if we can meet up for lunch or if I can pick them up right after school and go somewhere to talk. I have rarely had a life-and-death situation that could not wait. The promise of meeting soon gives them enough of a boost to get them through the night.

It is important to recognize your limitations. Jesus still spent time in the mountains praying while people suffered in the valley. You cannot save all your students, only God can! Many times, we try to rush in and wind up hindering the Spirit. Instead of students seeking God's work in their lives, they see you. Give God time to work. Pray and seek guidance. Follow that leading despite how uncomfortable it may seem. There is only one God and Savior, and we do not qualify as either one.

DISCIPLESHIP

(CHRIS POPE)

"Go therefore and make disciples …" this one aspect of ministry is weak in many churches today. We emphasize either on discipleship and forgo the evangelism aspect, or we are so seeker-friendly we are forcing students to receive nutrients off baby food. We need to *make* disciples. That cannot happen without evangelizing, and evangelizing is not successful without discipleship. Spiritual infants need cared for. I want to take a little bit of time to focus on the concept of discipleship and the direction I am coming from, and then we will talk about how to do this with the vast number of hours you have!

I remember the day my wife and I found out we were having a baby boy. I never felt an emotion in my life as the thought of holding my son in my arms. It felt official; I was going to be a daddy.

Of course, I had to get ready. I immediately began to prepare the house. I sat down with my wife and ordered his crib set. We picked the colors for his room and painted it the next day. By Sunday, I had his crib, changing table, newborn diapers, and wipes all prepared. Now, I had to wait another four months, but I was prepared.

The point I am trying to make is the importance of caring for an infant. I could not stand the thought of bringing a child home from the hospital without any preparation to care for him. I doubt you would either! So why do we not put the same care and concern into newborn Christians?

Discipleship is more than filling blanks in a book or reciting memory verses. It is life on life! I struggled with this as a part-time youth pastor. I am a Type A personality and wanted a plan and focus. I created my own material and researched other sources. I had a clear plan for getting disciples from point *A* to point *B*.

I actually found this was taking more time away from my family, and I was neglecting my primary responsibility. I started discipling seven students a week for up to two hours at a time. They wanted it, but they did not know what it could have looked like. Some of them, unfortunately, burned out.

I began to realize that I was trying to cram into six months what took the disciples three years to learn. I had to redefine my definition of discipleship. What is your definition of discipleship?

For my leaders, we defined discipleship as *the process by which people sincerely desire to actively rise to the next spiritual level, the goal being to become aware of their desired level of spiritual growth through their (1) thought process (pure mind), (2) action, (3) habits and disciplines, and their (4) lifestyle.*

Those four areas were where we saw the biggest deficit in the lives of our students. We sought to raise questions and get the students to think about their responses. We did not expect immediate results. Remember, this is a marathon and not a sprint. We need to remind ourselves and our students of this fact.

These became our goals.

- Pure Mind
  - o What does it mean to have a pure mind?
  - o What are you actively doing to keep your heart/mind pure?
  - o What are some things that you *know* are a stumbling block?
    - Books?
    - Movies?
    - Music?
    - Relationships?
    - Technology?
  - o What are you exposing yourself to (some of the above) that is hindering your spiritual growth?
  - o How does this affect your body and mind?
  - o What conversations are you participating in that is hindering your growth?
  - o What steps are you taking to grow?
- Action
  - o What do you think it means to live a transparent life?
  - o How transparent do you think you are?
  - o How do you respond to tense and stressful situations?
- Habits and Disciplines
  - o What habits/disciplines have you started to help you grow spiritually?
    - Quiet time?
    - Scripture memorization?
    - Spiritual disciplines?
  - o What habits do you need to change?
  - o What are some of the ways that you are applying what you are learning?

- Life gauges (similar to the ones for pastors)
  - o Physical
    - Are you keeping your body a temple of the Holy Spirit?
      - Food and drink
      - Exercise
      - Relaxation
  - o Spiritual
    - Spiritual disciplines
    - Bible study
    - Quiet time
    - Scripture memory

I know this sounds like a lot, but this was based on the needs of our students. This was planned with longevity in mind. We wanted them to grow slowly and retain what they learned. This was a model based in application and based in doing life together.

How can this be done with the time you have? The quick answer is you are not suppose to do it alone. This is a team effort with other students and leaders you have. I often find it funny how a student's peer can say the exact statement that I did and they *get it*!

To better manage your time and sanity, I recommend you reserve the one-on-one discipleship for the students who have major issues and the ones who are most invested into the ministry. These could be abuse, gender identity, social anxiety, etc. The rest of my students are discipled in a small-group setting.

Most attend the same school and are in similar grades. This allows them to build a network of growing and passionate Christian friends and influences that will build a natural accountability. You do not have to be the first person on speed dial. Take it as a compliment. You are reproducing yourselves in the lives of others.

Train your leaders! Your leadership team is a melting pot of various personalities, strengths, weaknesses, and stories. Train them to live life with your students. Help to point a particular leader to a student who is having a similar life experience so he or she is better equipped to help.

During my last ministry, I would have spent more time training leaders to disciple students. It is amazing when you reproduce yourself into a student to reach his or her generation, and imagine a team of adults doing the same in the lives of multiple students. Picture a leadership team each discipling three students who each do the same. Can you see the affect?

I also truly believe three is the magic number in discipleship. If you are bi-vocational, I would caution you to disciple no more than three students. Three is manageable and is not stealing you away from your family on a regular basis.

Earlier, I mentioned it was more than filling in a blank; it was living life together. How does this happen, and how can you effectively teach? I mix the two! I have a great resource I use in discipling students. It teaches them a variety of topics. It requires filling in the blanks, but it also enables practical applications.

I balance the lesson by having a hangout time the following week. This time can sometimes be an outing with my family or with the student. I plan this hangout time based on the topic we covered while allowing them to apply what they learned. For example, we will talk about speech and life and follow it up by attending a local basketball game to observe the actions and speech of those around. We note what is right and wrong and what the behavior communicates.

Some of the best conversations I have had with students centered on washing my car. We had a great time with the water, but they also felt safe to open up and talk. Many lives have been changed from doing something as simple as washing a car or building a picnic table. Let a student ride with you as you run errands or go to a store. In an age where students lack the ability to see healthy families, let them see you interact with your wife and kids. Them watching how you live the scripture is far more influential than you having them fill in a blank. Both are good, needed, and beneficial. Strike a balance. Do so in your life, their life, and in ministry.

WHEN TWO WORLDS COLLIDE

(CHRIS POPE)

This section was one of the main reasons we came together to write this book. There will be times in our ministry where our two worlds (two jobs) will collide. A battle is going to take place. Some of us work a secular job to supplement income, and many times the employer does not understand. I am going to share some experiences I have had in an attempt to give some direction and insight that you may be able to walk away with.

I have not always had to work a full-time job in addition to my church job. I always looked for part-time jobs that would compensate enough alongside my ministry work. I was very honest at the job interview; I explained who I was and what I did. Many times, the interviewee wanted to hear of my experiences, saw my level of passion and commitment, and desired those traits at the company.

My desire was to have several days of income in a savings account for those emergencies that popped up and needed my attention. These funds could cover my leaving due to an accident that either a student or parent was involved in, hospital visit, death, etc.

To be completely honest, very few emergencies will occur that your assistance is needed at that moment. There are times when it has, and my boss has always understood. I would typically use a portion of my vacation or sick time for such occasions, especially when I started to work full time in addition to my church responsibilities.

There is also the possibility a couple of leaders on stand-by could go to the hospital or scene of an emergency. Many of my female leaders were stay-at-home moms and could go at a moment's notice. College students can also be a lot of help since they often have some flexibility built into their schedules.

Most of my part-time jobs were with nonprofit organizations. They understood the needs of people in the community. They saw the importance of putting people first. They advocated what I was doing. Unfortunately, not every one of you is in that situation. I am sorry, as there are no quick answers or three-step processes to obtain the desired outcome. However, I want to encourage you. Remember your first love. Remember your calling. My calling is to be a Godly husband, father, and pastor—not follow the American dream.

I do not need everything the world tells me I need. Therefore, I do not need to pursue it. If I scale back, I can get by on less and still provide for my family. Do I still need a second job? Yes! Do I need to make as much to live? No! God has always provided what my family has needed and I still work hard.

My wife has always known my calling into ministry, and she would not have it any other way. She has never faulted me for responding to an emergency, even when were financially tight. But few situations have been emergencies that have required an immediate response.

Your two worlds will collide in many ways. Your preparation time, discipleship, evangelism, staff meetings, leadership meetings, youth group, trips, camps, retreats, etc., all collide because you are not a full-time youth pastor.

I hope the previous sections and chapters have given you useful tips and ideas on how to manage your time to avoid or properly navigate an emergency in your own life.

CONCLUSION

This book has been a joy to write. It has enabled us to reflect on our years in ministry and see how God has sharpened us into who we are today. We have made mistakes and many more are to come. We will look back at the end of our ministry days and will wish we had done some things differently, but still be able to rejoice that God's Word does not return void.

More than anything, I desire my students to have an Acts 8 experience. I am not talking about the scattering of the church, Simon the sorcerer, or even about being a eunuch. I want them to have the eunuch's heart and desire (Acts 8:31). It is amazing when a student wants to know more and seeks understanding. It is an emotional and joyous time when they respond. I want them to have a Philip.

I had the privilege of leading a student to Christ whom I did not know. He was visiting his cousin. I dropped them off at home and settled in for the night. I received a phone call about ten o'clock that night asking me if he could get baptized. I said, "Sure, what time would you like to meet?"

He responded, "Why not tonight?"

You have to love the excitement and transformation! This was a kid who could not wait to demonstrate to the world the choice he made for Christ. We found a pool that was open, and he publicly professed his faith in Christ.

I am sure this is the desire of your heart for your students. If this is the ministry you want—where there is interest, desire, response, and transformation—then let's do it first at home.

You have heard our hearts, and now it is time to act. You have read the stories of how we got to where we are and how we were molded. All of our experiences are different, but we serve the same God.

We hammered home the principle to remain balanced because you only get one family, and you are held accountable for how you lead them. Their view of God and church ministry depends a great deal on how you live.

Remember who it is that you serve! There are many churches, theological views, and ministry texts telling you how to conduct your ministry. Never forget who has called you! We serve the same King. Take what you hear, what you read, and seek His will. Trust and obey.

REFERENCES

This is a little extra help to guide you along the way. Here is a collection of references we have used over the years that have positively influenced our ministries. Neither of us have followed a specific model. We take what we learn and adapt it to the culture of our students and community. Not all of these texts are student friendly; however, you can make them so.

Planning / Organization/ Philosophy

Boshers, Bo. *Student Ministry for the 21st Century.* Grand Rapids, MI: Zondervan, 1997.

Burns, Jim. *Uncommon Youth Ministry.* Ventura, CA: Regal, 2001.

Fields, Doug. *Purpose Driven Youth Ministry.* Grand Rapids, MI: Zondervan, 1998.

—. *Your First Two Years in Youth Ministry: A Personal and Practical Guide to Starting Right.* Grand Rapids, MI: Zondervan, 2002.

Geiger, Eric, and Jeff Borton. *Simple Youth Ministry: A Clear Process for Strategic Youth Discipleship.* Nashville, TN: B&H Publishing Group, 2009.

Olson, Ginny, Diane Elliot, and Mike Work. *Youth Ministry Management Tools: Everything You Need to Successfully Manage Your Ministry.* Grand Rapids, MI: Zondervan, 2001.

Rainer, Thom, and Geiger. *Simple Church.* Nashville, TN: B&H Publishing Group, 2006.

Spiritual Disciplines

Foster, Richard. *Celebration of Disciplines: The Path to Spiritual Growth.* New York, NY: HarperCollins, 1998.

Henrichsen, Walter. *Disciples Are Made Not Born.* Colorado Springs, CO: Cook Communications, 1988.

Hughes, Kent, and Carey Hughes. *Disciplines of a Godly Young Man.* Wheaton, IL: Crossway, 2012.

White, John. *The Cost of Commitment.* Downers Grove, IL: IVP Books, 1976.

Whitney, Donald. *Spiritual Disciplines for the Christian Life.* Colorado Spirings, CO: NavPress, 1991.

Counseling

Clark, Chap. *Hurt: Inside the World of Today's Teenagers.* Grand Rapids, MI: BakerAcademic, 2004.

Gerali, Steven. *What Do I Do When Teenagers Deal With Death?* Grand Rapids, MI: Zondervan, 2009.

——. *What Do I Do When Teenagers Question Their Sexuality?* Grand Rapids, MI: Zondervan, 2010.

——. *What Do I Do When Teenagers Struggle With Eating Disorders?* Grand Rapids, MI: Zondervan, 2010.

McDowell, Josh, and Bob Hostetler. *Josh McDowell's Handbook On Counseling Youth: A Comprehensive Guide for Equipping Youth Workers, Pastors, Teachers, Parents.* Nashville, TN: Thomas Nelson, 1996.

Miller, Patricia, and Keith Miller. *Quick Scripture Reference for Counseling Youth.* Grand Rapids, MI: BakerBooks, 2006.

Parrott, Les. *Helping the Strugging Adolescent: A Guide to Thirty-Six Common Problems for Counselors, Pastors, and Youth Workers.* Grand Rapids, MI: Zondervan, 2000.

Van Pelt, Rich, and Jim Hancock. *The Youth Workers Guide to Helping Teenagers in Crisis.* Grand Rapids, MI: Zondervan, 2005.

Van Pelt, Rich, and Jim Hancock. *The Volunteer's Guide to Helping Teenagers in Crisis.* Grand Rapids, MI: Zondervan, 2012.

Discipleship

Barna, George. *Growing True Disciples.* Colorado Springs, CO: WaterBrook Press, 2001.

Holladay, Tom, and Kay Warren. *Foundations: A Purpose Driven Discipleship Resource.* Grand Rapids, MI: Zondervan, 2003.

MacArthur, John. *How To Study the Bible*. Chicago, IL: Moody Publishers, 2009.

——. *The Keys to Spiritual Growth; Unlocking the Riches of God*. Wheaton, IL: Crossway Books, 1991.

Neighbour, Ralph. *Student Survival Kit: An Essential Guide for New Christians*. Nashville, TN: LifeWay Press, 2007.

Putman, Jim. *Real-Life Discipleship: Building Churches That Make Disciples*. Colorado Springs, CO: NavPress, 2010.

Putman, Jim, Avery Willis, Brandon Guindon, and Bill Krause. *Real-Life Discipleship Training Manual: Equipping Disciples Who Make Disciples*. Colorado Springs, CO: NavPress, 2010.

Sanders, J. Oswald. *Spiritual Discipleship: Principles of Following Christ for Every Believer*. Chicago, IL: The Moody Bible Institute, 1994.

Swindoll, Charles. *The Owner's Manual for Christians: The Essential Guide for a God-Honoring Life*. Nashville, TN: Thomas Nelson, 2009.

Towns, Elmer. *A Beginners Guide to Reading the Bible*. Ann Arbor, MI: Vine Books, 2001.

——. *Understanding the Christian Life*. Virginia Beach, VA: Academx Publishing Services, 2005.

Printed in the United States
By Bookmasters